FROM OUTER NATURE TO INNER NATURE

A Journey In Awareness

JEFFREY T. CARL J. RAINBOW BEING

Balboa Press books may be ordered through booksellers or by contacting:

Balboa Press
A Division of Hay House
1663 Liberty Drive
Bloomington, IN 47403
www.balboapress.com
1 (877) 407-4847

ISBN: 978-1-5043-9194-8 (sc)
ISBN: 978-1-5043-9195-5 (e)

Library of Congress Control Number: 2019900038

Print information available on the last page.

Balboa Press rev. date: 03/25/2020

BALBOA.
PRESS
A DIVISION OF HAY HOUSE

FROM OUTER NATURE TO INNER NATURE

A Journey In Awareness

JEFFREY T. CARL J. RAINBOW BEING

From Outer Nature to Inner Nature

This is a journey of looking at the world from the outer beauty that lies around us in the natural world filled with many patterns, colors, and geometric shapes, to the inner nature that lies within and makes up our psyche, subconscious, higher consciousness, and inner realms.

We move into the center of the sacred flower of life, where all things spiral outward and inward throughout the multi-verse.

I will take you on my visual journey through the beauty of nature. When I look into the world around me, I notice more, I feel more, and I experience life in a more meaningful way.

As my senses open up, I look more deeply into nature and find myself transitioning from the outer visual nature to the inner visual nature. For me, it is a visual experience. For some, it may be an auditory experience, and for others it may be kinesthetic sensation throughout their bodies. We can experience all of these sensations to greater or lesser degrees.

For me, it is a visual experience. When I close my eyes, I also open up my eye.

Do we see only with our physical eyes? Do we see with our third eye? Or is it a blending of the left, right, and middle eyes, the outer and inner visions blending into one?

In this journey, I will take you on a visual quest through many shapes and images that have led me to the center of my heart and back again.

I am shown through images, colors, shapes, and geometry the connection to the flower of life, of which we are all a part.

The Journey Begins

As I enter the woods, the trees seem to move in a rhythmic dance, each becoming an individual being with its own persona.

The forest floor comes to life in many colors and shapes, each leaf in its own place, the colors becoming more and more vibrant.

The sounds seem overbearing with so many different noises—the bugs flying by, the birds sitting in the trees, the crickets in the grass.

The forest floor seems chaotic—fallen branches, new growth, old growth, rocks protruding from the moist soil.

I stop and take a few deep breaths. I smell the fragrance of decaying leaves, wet moss, and pungent fungi.

I leave the fast pace of city life behind me now, entering the woods more deeply. I breathe again and feel the air expanding my lungs and clearing out the stale air of the city left behind.

As I sit down on a fallen tree and look more deeply into the forest, the chaos seems to make way for more detailed order. I realize that the ferns and vines have a pattern to them, as do the trees, standing tall with their branches outstretched, reaching into the sky.

The flying bugs and the crawling bugs start to sound like a long, drawn-out conversation that I am unable to understand, broken only by the song of the birds.

I relax, and the forest opens up to me even more.

The stones become a trail to a deeper, clearer understanding of nature. The path leads me farther into the forest.

As I follow the trail of stones leading me farther into the woods, the forest clears away.

I come upon a stream and behold its majestic beauty. I breathe in and feel the fresh air filling my lungs.

As I sit and stare into the gently moving waters, the movement relaxes me and the sound of the waters calms my nerves, allowing me to release the tension in my body.

I gaze at a tree before me and notice the details in the bark, the shapes that make up the intricate patterns, the way the moss wraps around the trunk, drawing my attention to the rocks and leaves that make up the forest floor.

I breathe in deeply and release, enjoying the fresh air.

The colors become ever more alive, and the shapes of the stones and the leaves seem to hold within them a story, guiding me deeper into a feeling beyond my outer senses to a kinship with the world around me.

Behold, I see the face of nature's helpers peering back at me with a smile, beckoning me farther within myself and the woods around me.

I take another deep breath, and with a sigh, I move along with a more heightened sense of awareness.

I leave the stream and meander back to where the woods are denser.

I wander as though I'm being led by some unseen force, taking me here and there, and I don't pay any attention to where I'm going.

Suddenly I come upon a puddle in a depression of leaves and rocks.

I notice the reflection of the trees and the sky in the small body of water, as though it has become a mirror.

I sit down beside this pool and look more deeply into its reflective surface. I start to see through the outer reflection. I take a deep breath and become more peaceful in my mind, and my body becomes calmer.

I empty my head of thoughts that have been clouding my vision.

Like the pool, reflecting stillness at me, I become still.

I look for a moment at the leaves and rocks that frame the pool.

I notice the detail of the colors and shapes, how the dry faded leaves turn darker as they enter the water, becoming diffused in their own reflection.

Sitting there in the stillness, I take a long breath and release it, and the last of the tension in my body goes with it.

As I stare into the pool, my inner thoughts become less distracting. I look more deeply still into this tranquil water, not thinking about anything, just being at peace, empty for the moment of now.

My vision turns inward as I'm sitting by the calm pool.

The landscapes of my inner vision become more alive as the darkness subsides in my head.

As the inner visions come to life, I begin to see images of people in my life, some who still inhabit bodies and others who have passed through the veil.

Appearing hyper-real, they smile, and each one reveals to me a feeling through the expressions on their faces.

Some seem to pop out in my inner vision. I sit and enjoy this heightened experience with each one in turn.

Conversing with them seems so real … or is it?

In this state of awareness, those who have passed through the veil are alive and well again. I find myself enveloped in a deeper sense of love for all of them.

I notice one entity whom I haven't seen previously but who feels familiar to me.

Behind him, the colors seem to swirl in a rhythmic pattern, pulling me even further into my psyche.

"Allow me to help you see even more, my friend. Come deeper in, and you shall see something even more spectacular."

I breathe in and go further within my awareness, journeying deeper into consciousness.

While my eyes remain closed, I follow the color patterns of light and watch them swirl around my mind's eye. The colors dim as heavy thoughts move in, and I feel a sense of heaviness in my heart.

I have an awareness of knowing many different lives. The psychic impressions that I get of many people have tied me into a tapestry of kaleidoscopic images that weigh me down.

Remaining in this heightened state, I learn to forgive and let go. As I work through my feelings, I take another deep breath and release them in love.

To the left of my inner vision, I notice a glowing, feathery form. This being brings me a profound sense of calm.

As I give my attention to this being, my psyche begins to lighten, and the streams of heavy thoughts fade away.

Behind the illuminated form, another field of vision is appearing.

I make out new scenery and move my attention in that direction.

Suddenly the psychic visions move out of my head, and the feathery form shows me more of the natural world—an ethereal state of being.

A vision suddenly appears to me. The roots of the trees form a connection, each to the other, through an energetic field all around the earth.

In my heightened state, the trees communicate, by way of mental images to me, how all things are connected through them, the plants, fungi, and bacteria.

The trees are stationary beings bathing in the elements without moving from where they stand. Yet through their chemical and ethereal energy systems, they move their awareness around the world.

With a mental picture, the spirit of the trees communicates to me to be like them for a moment—incredibly still with no movement.

So I stand tall and become motionless.

I feel the wind gently caressing every hair on my exposed skin. As the wind dies down, my skin is charged with a tingling sensation. I feel this energy moving over my body, extending out all around me, slowly moving my hands close together but not allowing them to touch. I feel this energy moving between my fingers as a magnetic force. As I move my hands away from each other, ever so slowly, the energy between them becomes stronger. Gently extending my arms out as though they are branches of a tree, I feel the energy moving out from my heart, passing through my arms and outstretched fingers to the trees around me.

I feel a similar force of love from the trees, returning to me as I stand there, as still as they are.

Even without any movement, an incredible amount of energy is being moved.

I realize that both my outer eyes and my inner eye are open now. The world around me seems much more alive, and the colors and forms appear more vibrant with my heightened sense of awareness. The forest comes to life, and as I see with all three eyes, the world becomes even more beautiful.

The veil is lifted, and many worlds open up. Every being in this world has its place.

What once seemed chaotic is now an orchestra of life, sharing consciousness, colors, and sounds.

It takes me within the beauty of this place, as deep as I care to go into the story of the forest.

As my inner ear becomes more attuned to the sounds, I hear everything singing their own songs.

As I listen, it becomes clearer. I hear much, yet I understand only a little.

I feel connected to the world around me, from within the center of my heart, to the sacred flower of life that comes forth from within my heart, to all hearts in plants, minerals, and all beings, small and large.

From many dimensions of my human heart, this love flows out to you, the humans, the trees that I pass by in my daily life, and to myself.

This flower of life is expanding outward and inward at the same time.

OM AUM I AM OM

Slowly making my way from the pond and the tranquil place in my mind, with my senses heightened and a profound peace in my heart, I leave the woods.

I think of my home in the city, a small box in a larger box, with a small sleeping area that is my sanctuary.

I cross through the veil of clamor that the city holds—the right angles, the hard lines of the buildings, the loud sounds of the city streets. The psychic energy that moves in currents throughout the avenues is all very different from the gentle feeling of the woods, which is now deep inside me. Is it better or worse?

To me, it's just different, each holding its own magic. If you will only look, you will see.

I adjust myself and filter through the diverse energies that make up the city.

I notice each building and look to the windows, at the light that each one holds within.

I have many impressions of the thoughts and feelings of all the people, floating out into the streams of psychic energy that move in currents around us.

I go inside to the living altar that I created in my window with lots of plants, stones, water, and fire. I give thanks for each day and feel unending gratitude for what this life brings to me.

It is a comfortable place I have created here, with everything I need. I adjust to the changes, lying down in the sanctuary of my bed, calming my senses, continuing the journey within.

I find myself in the comfort of my bed, in the room that I created for myself to lie in peace. As I lie here and feel the warm covers and softness of my pillow, I relax and feel secure for now in a peaceful state of contentment. I notice my body and feel the energies around and inside me.

There are many different ways to play with this energy and bring myself into a state of peace.

I choose to wrap this energy around my body in a spiral, and I visualize it as many different colors. I move it by way of mental thought from my feet to the top of my head, slowly spiraling around my body, around each leg and each arm. Then I move the energy from the top of my head back down to my feet.

This enables me to notice if I have any chakras out of alignment or if any of my meridians are clogged. By doing this, I also notice when the energy stops flowing.

A sudden thought: who I am thinking about, and what story am I playing? Then I stop and say, This is my time. I send a peaceful violet flame of transmutation to all who are involved and to myself.

I breathe love into the spot in my body that is in distress.

Feeling free, I then activate the chakras by color. This creates a rainbow tunnel so that I can leave this dimension and move a little farther in.

By now my body is relaxed to the point of a nice, comfortable numbness that engulfs me.

As I lie in this relaxed state, I do another exercise.

The inner I takes the outer me deeper into the astral plane by self-hypnotizing.

The inner I starts to slowly count backward from ten to one, as if the outer self is a client of the inner therapist self.

I find that this works best when I am fully relaxed and can let myself go ever so deep until the feeling of a story takes over. Maybe it is a trail that leads me down a path, and I discover a secret garden or a door that opens up, and I find myself in my beautiful healing sanctuary. Beautiful symphonies can be heard throughout my being with melodies that carry me on wings of love and rhythms that match my heart, a beat in time with my soul. What we can experience is endless.

As I see through the darkness in my mind, the swirling lights move in a hypnotic spiral, taking me deeper as I count, "Seven, six, five …"

Moving deeper into my subconscious, I continue, "Three, two, one …"

As my inner eye opens, the astral planes come into view. With an explosion of color, shape, and patterns, I go further within to just the right place to move more deeply within my subconscious.

As the journey continues, I realize the power that lies within.

As I lie still, colors swirl around in my inner vision.

When I try to focus on one pattern, it seems to fade back into the darkness, only to reappear just out of sight as a ball of color, many colors, all moving along in a rhythmic dance.

As I relax more and look without looking, something clicks. I go further into the colors.

I make out these shapes as spirals and stars that lead me deeper into this mesmerizing pattern.

What are these shapes and colors trying to reveal to me?

While focusing my attention in this space, I perceive untold universes all moving through darkness.

As I remain still, my attention returns to my body, and for a moment everything is darkness again.

A calming feeling enters my awareness, my body is relaxed, and my mind is at rest.

Off to the side of my inner vision, the ball of color appears. I notice some forms trying to come forward. I look deeper into the shapes again, but they disappear into the darkness.

My body needs to move, so I adjust myself and focus my attention on resuming my inner journey.

Through the darkness, I get a glimpse of the colors as they begin to form more detailed shapes.

The circles, rectangles, and squares come together.

I wonder what these shapes mean. Are they atoms, molecules, cells, other forms of ethereal filaments of light, or points of internal astral light?

Again the scene changes, alternating between moments of color and moments of no color.

Remaining calm, I let the scene unfold again in my inner vision. I am completely relaxed with my head as empty as possible.

The colors return, brighter and with more form. They come together in what appears to be an image.

Maybe it's just my imagination, though it is said that everything originates in the imagination. I allow my imagination to create what it wants as I lie there focusing my attention on the images that appear to me … before they disappear again.

The vision comes to me, bringing understanding—through my intuition—as the different scenes unfold their meanings to me.

I journey further into the inner nature of my being.

I get up and move around, bring life back into my body after being deep inside.

Continuing my journey by going to the outer world, I grab my paints and brush and sit down to draw.

I let the images emerge from my inner guidance.

The pencil moves on its own, and the image starts to form.

A face emerges from the swirling patterns spiraling out from my brush, forming rectangular cells in brown, tan, blue, pink, and golden hues blended together.

Pathways of yellow light mark out directions leading into the distance, as the being becomes clearer in the center of the patterns.

All paths lead to this center, spiraling through this shape.

I sense from this figure that all points of movement through its being move both inwardly and outwardly.

I understand that this being is an energetic life force, controller of time and destiny.

Do you know that the cosmic mother has many helpers, who work in many different ways?

Even what appears to be just energy or a pattern has an inner consciousness.

I find that the white and black universe mean a lot to me.

I am shown how patterns and shapes can mean more than can be expressed with words.

The movement of lines takes us further on our inner journey.

The next vision I get is from the mental realm.

This is where I see rational thought aligned into compartmentalized segments of beliefs, structured to create long, drawn-out thoughts built upon its rational self, creating multiple time lines flowing simultaneously.

There is a zero point of alignment where all things come together and move forward as a unified timeline, bringing forth our free will in balance with the heartfelt flow of our creator, encompassing the wisdom of time creating no-time.

Bring forth our unified will for the good of all.

It's our time that moves us along in a golden way as the journey continues in the moment of now.

As my inner vision expands, I further my journey into inner space. I stare at the blank paper and let my hands move my brush freely. The center comes out first, swirling green and blue lines that spiral in a Möbius strip within itself. I feel this to be our earth plane through a more etheric state.

I get the impression that each dot comes forth as a color, and as I place dots in random patterns, my attention is drawn to the angelic realm, where higher mental and compassionate thoughts pour in.

As I place each dot, it becomes a seraphim, angelic host, soul companion, or guardian angel. For each and every human, there is a heavenly host. How do these dots transform into angelic hosts? Maybe only in my imagination. As I place each dot, my vision increases and I see telepathic images in my head and feel a sense of peace in my heart.

I get these downloads from my higher self showing me that a legion of angels and celestial beings are all around us, showering us with their guidance of love and inspirational insights, to help us be free in our daily lives.

They help us become true children of earth, free to create in love and respect, with the blessing of our creator within. We are all children of creation, so let us create. My soulful self lets me know that "angels are the eyes and ears of the creator" and that we humans are "the feet and hands of the creator." Each of us travels through the different dimensions and experiences of life, feeding this information back to the center of all things where our father and mother of creation abide.

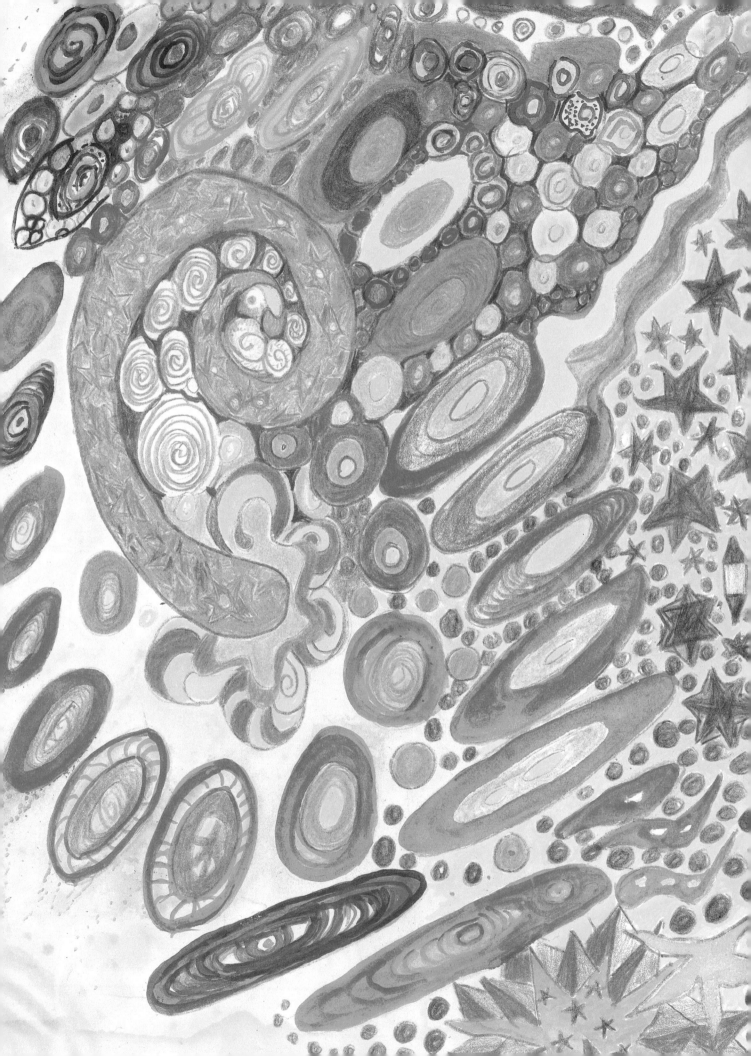

I am also shown the triangles of Trinitized teacher-spirits coming into our dimension through explosions of insight and inspiration.

Bringing us practical insight, they bathe our human minds with illumination and visions, so that we can make our world more like the heavenly world around us.

I see diamond patterns of crystalline uplifters coming to upgrade our energetic bodies as we expand our sensitivity and become even more aware of the world around us.

These visions of energies come into my mind when I open up to an expanded viewpoint of my inner sight. I find myself transitioning more deeply into my soul consciousness, being shown more of the realms of love and light and how they play out in many forms.

As I become more attuned to my inner vision, I see the dots transforming into many different forms and distinct shapes.

I see Mer-Ka-Ba beings of pure light, star seeds, and hexadecimal crystal fields as the colors and shapes become beings of light in form, coming to assist us from the realms of light.

The beings of the violet flame bring forth their great ray of transmutation.

I see balanced orbs of light and the souls of many enlightened beings sending their light to their counterparts here on outer earth.

I see this great outpouring of love from the cosmic mother flowing in a spiral to the outer world and awakening our hearts.

I am made aware of my light body through my inner vision, and I feel my own energy field wrapping around me in a more tangible way.

Now the journey moves me further in and further out.

I feel my energy body around me, and I can perceive my light body. As my outer and inner vision becomes unified, I notice an orb of light around me.

I become more kinesthetic and notice that my thoughts and feelings have weight and color. As they move around my energy body, I feel the celestial energies from beyond my crown chakra passing through my head, down my neck, and into my heart where my *I am* presence, the creator's spark, merges with this force. This active force moves from my cranium to my sacrum, extending from the tip of my spinal cord, through my root chakra, down my legs, and out through the soles of my feet.

I then ground this energy deep in the heart of Gaia.

As Gaia gently sends back her kundalini energy, it enters my body through my feet and rises up through my legs into my root chakra. There it energizes my sacral chakra and moves to activate my pubic center. As this living, sensual, loving energy moves throughout my body, it brings this life force to my energy system and physical body.

I feel a balance between the masculine and feminine within my body.

As I draw forth the energy that surrounds me, I co-create a union between heaven, earth, and myself.

I create a connection to my light body and begin the activation.

How a person experiences their own light body is personal. I am describing how my energies move through me.

The energy field around us and inside us is an area of lifelong study. I am giving you only a small glimpse into what I see and feel around me.

The path to inner awareness is worth spending time on. It is a truly never-ending, always expanding journey. We continue to go more deeply within!

As I open my heart chakra, allowing the male/female energies to move through my body, I pull the energies up through all my energy centers and back into my heart.

Here I balance the energies with the divine flame of love as I move more deeply into the center of my heart, where the outer layers of the flower of life appear to me. This vision is how my sacred flower of life opens to me. The sacred flower in each person's heart will open to them in their own way.

As I allow myself to feel and I draw this flower of life, I blend the feminine and masculine energies together. My twin flame is all around me, or perhaps I could say that my soul is my twin flame. The true union happens within the heart for each self with their soul.

As the flower unfolds, I see lines of yellow life force moving through its center, blending the female and male energies in a union of love.

Each circle takes me deeper into the center of the blue flower of my heart, surrounded by the flames of the creator mother's love.

As I go more deeply within, by her grace she reveals more to me.

Through images and visions of love and light, I receive an understanding that comes from within.

I journey deeper into the blue flower in my heart.

It opens up its petals to reveal the seed of life deeper within my heart.

As the threefold flame blends the blue, pink, and yellow lights together, they resonate in a beautiful geometric point of consciousness in the center of my heart, where the spark of the creator abides.

This spark of the creator that lies in the center of all things, which lies in the center of everything

It is this spark, the light of the creator, that ignites the waves of love to vibrate throughout our bodies, by way of our hearts, through our blood to nourish our cells.

As I meditate on this pattern, I experience a calming yet energetic feeling. The colors and lines seem to move as various patterns appear and disappear.

Although this is only a vision on paper, I take this image and visualize it within my heart. As I meditate on this fractal of sacred geometry, it expands my consciousness through the portal of my heart.

Feeding my body, this orgasmic energy further opens the portal of my pineal gland with her sweet kundalini love.

She nourishes my pituitary gland, the center of the lotus flower in my crown, which showers me in multicolored rainbow light, feeding the light to each chakra.

I receive further pictures within this light language as the journey continues.

My mind's eye fills with images of circles or eggs of consciousness. As the eggs of life swirl around in a spectrum of visual light, orbs of pure possibility present themselves to my outer vision with the help of water and color. I bring the feeling from my heart and through my hands, allowing the vision to appear on the paper in front of me.

I sit and meditate on the gyroscopic blue and fuchsia image, which appears to be a compass directing me to an inner portal. As I am surrounded by a yellow sea of quantum light, the points of light transform into the elements that make up our world.

The eggs of life transform into the seed thoughts of light, creating the four elements.

The circles swirl around, and the base square appears from the centers of the flowers, creating the earth we walk upon.

Some seeds expand into flowers and become triune, creating perfect triangles in balanced, vibration sequences of geometric flowers of air.

Other seeds blossom into rounder, more flowing flowers that move in endless swirls, spinning this way and that with a watery fluid motion.

Still others crystallize into more refined patterns. This refined, creative fire of concentration brings forth its gemlike nature. We are refined in pure light, tempered by the flames of our pure hearts, and balanced in our pure thought.

As I view this from the center, the portal of my soul, the passageway is unlocked and I see the word from my soul's eye.

The journey continues.

From this center within our beings, the creative mother-teacher brings to light for us the gardens that we create as we become the flowers of our lives.

We allow our souls' tones to vibrate our bodies, minds, and hearts into the intricate patterns of the beautiful flowers that we become.

We see that each of us is as unique as a snowflake, yet no two of us are alike.

We see how feeling the beating of our hearts connects us to the rhythm that flows throughout life.

We see how people come together to form bouquets of beautiful flowers.

Each person is unique, as we come to know ourselves as true children of creation.

The mother/father creator is the gardener who plants the seeds of life throughout creation. We humans are seeds from this creative force. The mother/father of love and light lives in each of us; we are their children. The universe, as a conscious being, experiences life through us.

As we experience life through the universe within and outside ourselves, together we are the garden.

So the journey moves us full circle as we swirl around and around.

The spiral of infinity lies before and behind us, above and below us, to our left and right.

The future isn't written in stone, for it is what we make of it.

Well, I hope that I have shed a little light on some dimensions that we as multidimensional human beings can explore.

As you close the book and return to the world outside, may you notice more and let yourself discover the mysteries inside and outside your being.

May you become your own gardener as you watch the enfolding of your sacred flower within your heart.

May you create your garden within and around yourself for all of your delights.

In love and light, I bid you farewell

Jeffrey T. Carl J. Rainbow Being

Printed in the United States
By Bookmasters